Grave Unknown

Ruby Wednesday

BookLeaf Publishing
India | USA | UK

Presentation by *BookLeaf Publishing*

Web: www.bookleafpub.com

E-mail: info@bookleafpub.com

ISBN: 9789357445092

First edition 2021

For the Fools,

Still looking for moments of magic.

Acknowledgment

My deepest gratitude for those who have unconditionally supported me; and the ones who did not. You have all been inspirational.

Preface

I have always been captivated by the cosmic symbolic Universe of the Tarot and have consistently been inspired by the windows into another world beyond our own.

Tarot first drew me in one lonely day in the library in school. Ostracised by peers, I sought solace within the bookshelves and I have been researching and working with the Tarot ever since my school days.

The cards themselves have their own copious stories to tell and I have begun to scribe my own within these poems with the comfort of their ever-presence.

I

Slick, sharp blades
Tumble from your bloodied tongue
Falling into a haphazard pile
In my cupped hands

Beautiful words scrawled
Upon each tiny mirror
In romantic cursive,
Crimson ink

There is a power in you
That terrifies me
There is a power in you
That repulses me

We all have an ability
And we all have a devilry
That chews, that devours
In our own personal abyss

Though
It is our decision
Which one we allow
To consume us

II

Knelt before your gracious silence
With the waves lapping at the shore
Salted air stinging my tear-filled eyes
A ruby fruit resting in my hands
Honed fingernails pierce the fruit's flesh
Liquor bleeding into the creases of my palms
Tearing through the flesh of the crimson orb
And shove fistfuls of seeds into my salivating mouth

The corner of your lip curls slowly upward
The fruit destroyed and myself created
And when I look upon you it is my face reflected
With wry smile gazing back at me
Smothered in garnet-stained juice

III

Brittle limbs, a snapped body
A quiet decomposition amongst
The undergrowth
Consumed by nettles, fern and thorn

Peaceful, dying

In the damp
Hungry spores breed
Take root and expand; viral
Spreading gracefully

Consuming life, becoming life
A silent rotted burst of being
From the decay. Warm, moist decay
That chews rapidly through flesh

Birthed, created
Killed, destroyed

Through this fallen Silver Birch
Humble mycelium breeds
Sprouting polypore, shank and bonnets

There is new life after death
There is new life within death

IV

A delicately steaming black coffee
Presented in porcelain cup and saucer
A perfect tarry blend of bitter sweetness
An appreciative exhale from the first
Blackened sip; tendrils of breath curling
From my throat and my tongue content

And you.
Your perfectly placed, poised posture
Behind open grand piano; secure, strong, square
You play the greats, some contemporaries,
Meandering through humid summer Iris gardens
And ponder upon things to work on

A cigarette hissing in a leaf-shaped ashtray
The sunlight piercing through the glass doors
Catching a singular blue-tinted stream of smoke
Curling toward the ceiling
Harsh against the searing, pink lilies
Rivalling your morning grapefruit

Abandoned Malbec litters the room and
I gaze upon last night's rouge port
Rhythmically oscillate inside a slight chalice
As you strike keys, I place a kiss upon your
crown

Running my fingers through your hair
Your beard and across your chest

Opened mouthed and opened eyed kisses
And suddenly, I am not so secure
I feel I miss you already

V

Youth, Father and Sage
Bathe in your worship as you sleep, child
Whilst Maiden, Mother and Crone dwindle
Yet wait for you patiently, child
Waiting to welcome you home

Your teachers are lying to you, child
You must consume their knowledge
You must hear and you must listen to everything
Yet, of upmost importance, child
You must question that and
You must question them
You must question what you are reading right now, child
You must question every single word that you read
Every utterance that you hear
The grandeur is to tempt you from the doorway, child
To distract you from the keys

Youth, Father and Sage
Bathe in your worship as you sleep, child
Whilst Maiden, Mother and Crone dwindle
Yet wait for you patiently, child
Waiting to welcome you home

VI

Taken by a dropped surprise
Tension on my neck, as I
Am informed of a great escape
My mouth engulfed with bitter taste

The creases sit around the eyes
However much that you despise
The constant state of belligerence
Left a pool of abandoned compliments

Upon the furrowed brow I sit
A soft connection from dry lips
Like the one upon your neck
Fractions of skin that I inspect

The brief moments that will sit with me
Will be the ones where it was seen
At that tenderness of crumbled walls
A confession, where the words would fall

Tumbled from the very teeth
That once kept those secrets safe and deep
A subtle pain where my head will sit
That same place where so did my lips

VII

My shell was once impervious
And I was once so delicate inside
That shield has slipped now
Morphing, swapping
My outsides feel softer now
Vulnerable, I am
My armour weakened
My skin peeled away
Where the tiniest of breezes
Prickle my exposed nerves

My exterior shed
And now I must wait
In order for this new sheath to crystallise
Keeping you out
And everything of mine in
Perhaps then I can continue
Continue to venture, to stray
Uncover somewhere new, though
For now, I am brittle
For now, I am hiding

VIII

Give me the strength
To pull back the bedsheets and expose my pallid skin to the cool air

Give me the strength
To dress and drag my body to the kitchen to make the coffee

Give me the strength
To resist smoking an unnecessary cigarette

Give me the strength
To stop zombie-like scrolling and put my phone down

Give me the strength
To pick the phone up when someone calls

Give me the strength
To not text him

Give me the strength
To not look at old photographs and reminisce over good times with bad people

Give me the strength

To not text him again

Give me the strength
To make myself, no matter how pitiful,
something to eat

Give me the strength
To only take the suggested dose

Give me the strength
To shower, brush my teeth and feel the breeze
caress my skin and fill my lungs

Give me the strength
To not lose control in front of them and keep the
cracks from breaking open

Give me the strength
To not push the intolerable in front of cars, buses
or trains

Give me the strength
To not cry in front of these strangers

Give me the strength
To smile at the appropriate people

Give me the strength

To look at a to-do list and not be so
overwhelmed with the smog in my mind

Give me the strength
To not jump

Give me the strength
To keep my eyes open before stepping into the road

Give me the strength
Please give me strength to get out of bed

IX

A single red light
In an otherwise vacuous darkness
Inspect your palms
Watch your folding fingers
Study the creases carved into the flesh

A hollow wind groaning through
A copious vacancy
The longing heartbreak for no one
Grief seared into your breast
The sadness, the absence

Is anyone out there?
Am I singing to an empty room?
Even these self-indulgent passages
Left folded and unread
Pressed inside these pages

X

Our time is not linear, friend
The face of a clock is no two-dimensional circle
Time is cyclical, yes
Only from the perspective in which we perceive it
We, in truth, stare into a gateway to a tunnel of time
Not a circle; we stare into a continuous spiral
The hands will wind around the image
And return to a point that appears original

That time is no longer yours
We have progressed through this time
Further into the tunnel
We're on a new wrung of this spiral

We have endured
We have suffered
We have grown
We have aged

Does time only exist
Because of the existence of death?

XI

Cast your blindfold eyes
Across the city
With back turned upon Saint Paul
Grasping on to diplomacy and reality
Evermore faced from the dogmatic production
of
A crucifix-lecherous boys' club
Remaining impartial to the
Falsehoods of the church
And now, Themis,
I fear it is too late
I fear you have turned your back on us all

XII

Today I saw where a man's last moments
occurred
Stray creepers crawled inside his shed
Through the cracks underneath the door
Searching for the one who nurtured them
Reaching up to the ceiling to pull him down
Release a trapped soul from its confines

An upturned mug, to me
The most harrowing souvenir
The passing of durational chaos, a torturous
struggle
A trusty companion, quenching thirst
As he would look upon his land
Across his kingdom
Perhaps the only thing he felt he had left

I wonder
If the flowers fear their inevitable demise
If the plants feel it time for them to cease
I am, of course, aware that it is cyclical
But we fear the end of ours, do we not?
I wonder if they have an awareness of the
approach of
The end
And if they were to mourn
When Death has swept by

XIII

Amongst the bleak stillness
I stare into what was once a recognisable face
Perhaps not so dissimilar to my own
Or, maybe, there was never a time before
Born promptly in to death

It's quiet here
I can see why you may like it
It must be pleasant here for you
As the breeze whips around the fabric draped
around your frame
Whistling through empty eye sockets
I wonder what we're doing here

Occasionally we will join
And every so often, I think you appear to show
A moment of what's to come
To stare Death in the face, though
Death doesn't look back
So, neither should we

XIV

The putrefying waters
That we have pissed in
The Mother intoxicated with
Poisons that we cast into her

Kept inebriated, kept submissive
She must not sober
She must remain half-cut
And subservient

If she were to sober
The rivers will begin to run backward
Waterfalls will begin to climb
Back up the mountainside

The oceans drained
The life below suffocated
Leaving vast barren gashes in the Earth
Where the Seven Seas once raged

No more flowers
No more fruit
No more meat
No more

One of these days
She will take it back

XV

The bruising on my throat from the noose of
chains
Wrenching me back into position if I would
wander
Wrists worn raw and bleeding from incessant
blind puppetry
Whilst you remind me to love myself and
To not accept mistreatment from the wretched
world
To be relentlessly and unapologetically myself;
to an extent
Yet, when the mask slips
And I see what lurks behind
It was you
All along, it was you
You were the beast
These chains are loose
These chains were always loose, how tragic
Knowing I could've left at any moment
Abandoned you in your own twisted darkness
Your words, your curses and self-indulgence
That incarcerated me, enslaved by serpent
silver-tongued deceit
Your aching hunger for superiority
Importance, adoration, devotion
I understand

I understand that I had my uses to you
Just another sentient doll stuffed with voice box
Crammed with what you yearned to hear
Full of strenuous, relentless doting words
For you to pull, release and revel in manipulated praise
The batteries now long dead
And no matter the nuanced exploitations
Tactics of brute-like threats built from suppressed rage
So quick to switch to bargaining when the former would fail
Fortunately, that person you once knew is long dead
I buried them myself

XVI

So full of fear
We are all so full of fear
It's only really the unknown that we are truly afraid of

Something we do not comprehend
Something we fail to get our heads wrapped around

The breeze whips through my hair
As I stare toward the ground below me
From my window over the treetops and beyond
I am not afraid of the falling
I am not afraid of the brief flying freedom
It is beyond that freedom; what comes after

If I were to shift my weight
Let go of the carpet at my feet
And teeter through the glass
I would soar
I would soar to the ground
Strike the earth like lightning
Smashing straight through the concrete
The dirt, the filth, the worms, the dead
Continue into an unknown beyond
Somewhere quiet and painless

Or somewhere torturous and violent
Or nothing
Endless nothing
Human megalomania creating a pointless afterward
Obsessive compulsion that ourselves must continue

So full of fear
We are all so full of fear
It’s only really the unknown that we are truly afraid of

XVII

Look toward the dark sky
The vastness of unfathomable space
The vastness of lost time; dead time
Between you, between us, between them

Lay for a humbling moment
Watch Sirius scorch and drift
Amongst the fields of the night
Orion calling to him during the hunt

XVIII

The silver rays of the Harvest Moon
Flood into the corners of my bedroom
You are quick to chase your brother this time of year
As you dance around us, painting spirographs across the Heavens
Ensnaring the Earth in a cosmic spiderweb

I'll leave my curtains pulled open for you
I have no desire to prevent you
From visiting during and beyond
The twilight hours. Please,
Protect me as I slumber; slay the sprites
That toy with my dreams until your brother's return

XIX

As golden and as radiant as you are
Cradling lyre and quiver crowded with divine
quarrel
Bewitching my mind, wound my soul
Filling me with poetry, music and
Gifts of sight beyond human means

A soft scent of hyacinth lingers from your pores
I kiss a silver tear that slowly trickles down your
chalked face
Fingernails caress your scalp to your nape
You pull closer and our lips would meet
Entwined within you, still and radiant amongst
woodland whispers
Energetic conversation between you and I
And the life around us, striving to obtain
connection
For us to feel less abandoned within the spaces
between
My gratitude to the archer, in hopes I too remain

XX

What are you doing here, dead boy?
I put you in the fucking ground
And left you behind
For good reason

XXI

Calm your mind here
It is never truly over
We can begin again
Whenever we need
We have an eternity here
Turn your insides out and
Welcome the transcendent syzygy
Steal moments to dance with yourself
With every aspect of yourself, our selves
You have permission

Take it with you, or start again

www.ingramcontent.com/pod-product-compliance
Lightning Source LLC
Chambersburg PA
CBHW051754130826
49812CB00033B/1145
9789357445092